THE RIVAL

THE AGHA SHAHID ALI PRIZE IN POETRY

The
Rival

Sara Wallace

THE UNIVERSITY OF UTAH PRESS

Salt Lake City

AGHA SHAHID ALI

PRIZE IN POETRY

The Agha Shahid Ali Prize in Poetry
Series Editor: Katharine Coles
Advisory Editor: Paisley Rekdal

The Defiance House Man colophon is a registered trademark of the University of Utah Press. It is based on a four-foot-tall Ancient Puebloan pictograph (late PIII) near Glen Canyon, Utah.

19 18 17 16 15   1 2 3 4 5

Library of Congress Cataloging-in-Publication Data

Wallace, Sara, 1967-
  The rival / Sara Wallace.
    pages cm. -- (The Agha Dhahid Ali Prize in Poetry)
  ISBN 978-1-60781-423-8 (pbk. : alk. paper)
  ISBN 978-1-60781-424-5 (ebook)
1. Women--Poetry. 2. Marriage--Poetry. 3. Motherhood--Poetry. I. Title.
  PS3623.A44385R58 2015
  811'.6--dc23
                                        2014049403

Cover image by Leon Harris, © iStock.com

Contents

THE RIVAL

I.

IT IS BEAUTIFUL

—after Jules Supervielle

It is beautiful to have seen the electric wires
slice the sun setting into sixths
with all the locusts like plums
bleeding against the dark trees,

to have once entered that red maple
and to have watched cars pass from its boughs,

to have stayed when you beat me
and then to have been freed
into a night as warm as skin.

It is beautiful to feel the body engorge
and to understand, even though seconds
are something like apples I hold,
these are not mine.

It is beautiful to get so drunk
and drive over hills over bridges
under which a tarry water shudders.

It is beautiful to know my body
(which walks me to buses and nightclubs
and over to my lover eating octopus)
is walking into a thin chill shade,
the oblong shadow of a narrow tower,
down that skinny carless alley.

It is beautiful to have been shown the whole pattern,
like a rug spread out on a woman's arm,
then to choose the one with small black squares,
so coarse when I bundle it up,
like holding an armful of biting spiders.
I spread it out all over my living room floor
and I sit on it, and select words.

LET ME BLINDFOLD YOU

This is whispered, hissed. My room turns the color of a wrinkle on a black skirt. I smell rain. The windows must be open. What do you look like? You sound like power lines, the signal I only hear when I'm alone. I reach out. Mouth like a wet warm hillside. Mushroom-slick skin. Like woods. Moist ground. Rain on the leaves. *My hands, please*, I say. *Tie them*. Nothing happens for a long time. You could be getting rope. You could be putting your jeans on. Have twenty years gone by? I feel lamplight warm on my thigh, like a tongue.

EDGE

the tongue pulled out of the phone

let me tell you how I'm feeling *fuck if I know*

lighting an American Spirit on the sauce splattered stove

such numbness is also a way of driving things underground

I'm going right to the edge I want to see those jagged rocks

when they said *you can have a normal life on lithium* I laughed

I'm going to take this as far as I can

there really is a dove on the phone line

my cat's whole body quivers and she's never even been outside

BLACK IRIS
—after a line by Robert Hass

I think *black iris the perfect metaphor for sexual evil* having seen this tall flower
that wasn't black and wasn't an iris but was purple as a mouth under neon

nipples brown as pennies on your flat chest

you lie in red boxer shorts in an unmade bed you're dipping pretzels in peanut
butter and watching the Pacers and talking to your mom on the phone

I'm across the river in another city a long train ride away leaning over the fire
escape watching cars on the BQE

blond and red ribbons of moving light

maybe it's not the flowers that look that way but the fence they're against
rusted wrought iron spiked and crooked leaves spent sunflowers

across the street a light comes on a woman stands in the sink in a yellow
bathrobe a moth's shadow on the wall behind her

when I first visited your studio I washed my hands in the sink and saw days
old condoms in the trash like pearly worms

I think *black iris the perfect metaphor for sexual evil* having seen this tall flower
that wasn't black and wasn't an iris but was purple as a mouth under neon

what if before I wrote *heart* or *penis* or *newspaper* I had to be responsible for
those words what if I owed them something

Blind Date

You told me to dress up. A necklace of black mirrors. I hiked my skirt up past my knees. *Sit down*, you said. Goblets. Charred steak on gilded plates. I was all mons, a quivering bowl of blood wrapped in silk and stubble.

Then I crawled panting across the clay sheets.

Your underwear lay on the dirty floor with the crickets, lit by the bent finger of the moon.

White Gold

rue the day

rue the bed

rue the worn sheets

rue the stars above my head

Prettier than platinum but not as strong, the salesgirl said. *Pick careful. You're going to wear it forever and you don't want no regrets.*

rue the headlights yellowing my walls

rue your beauty a walled garden

rue your pliant skin

rue your pliant lies

rue your face a bank of daisies sparkling and always bending in the wind

rue Donna the middle-aged woman you first stole from

rue Samantha *it's not using* you said *it's utilizing*

rue Terry *she follows me around like a puppy*

rue Robert the rich man who called the one who said *there's something you need to know*

rue the others I don't know their names

rue thinking you didn't sleep with them

Hush, you said. The smell of rotting greens and new mint from the open window, your tongue fused to my ear.

rue New Orleans

rue Bourbon

rue Royal

rue Burgundy

rue the live oak

rue loveliness slippery and humid

rue every dollar you left by the bed

rue the leather string adorned with animal bones you wore tucked under your shirt to the bank rue your secret in a knot of skin

You said, *The leaves never die here, they just fall.*

rue pulling the blinds shut all the time

rue deer bones in the back of the pickup truck

rue the gun I dreamed about using

rue driving down Oracle the levee like oven walls

planes and stars lit like electrical coils

Your ex-girlfriend said, *He gets in you gently but he gets in so deep.*

rue the power plants red on the river

rue Cancer Alley

rue crocodiles rippling the black water

rue Chartres

rue Ponce de Leon

Rue de la Course Café—

de la course the course of my life

rue thinking *oh, that was just talk*

Oh, that little blob where we cut the ring to size? The salesgirl said, *You can just turn it around and no one will ever know it's there.*

I called up your mama and I said *I guess the apple doesn't fall far from the tree*

I called up your dad and he said *it sure causes a lot of pain but it makes the ol' world go round*

I called up the state attorney's and someone said *we can mail you xeroxes of the forgeries*

she said *do you want to press charges*

she said it didn't surprise her at all

rue not asking when you changed your name again

City Courthouse Orleans Parish

rue words set to music

rue the needle stuck in the groove

rue the sheer nightie your mother gave me for Christmas

every woman needs something beautiful she said

BLUE CURVE OF EMPTY INTERSTATE

neon puddles, ghostly gas stations
gliding midnight, limousine
your hand on the steering wheel

patches of black ice
patches of snow phosphorescently lit
brand new wedding rings

your skin white as salt under the domed roof light
cooler full of wrecked cake, diaphragm, pint of rum
we were certain

I forgot to feed you cake at the wedding
I forgot about the photographer
no flower girl saddening in sherbet frill

blue tongues flickering over the oil refinery plant
we arc into the dark
talk to me, you said, *I don't want to fall asleep*

You

You are a fool. You spread your fingers when you talk and lift your hands in naked joy and your enthusiasms are as thick as falling rain. This makes me love you.

You are a user. You feel people up for what they're worth like a drunk pinching a just-found wallet in an empty parking lot. This makes me want to be loved by you.

You're so cold. You creak back in your chair, eyeing the glitter and spackle on the ceiling, the fly-thick dome covering the lightbulb, saying, *Time for you to go now*. This makes me want to spread myself out for you like a fawning necklace seller spreading his hippie beads out on slippery fabric at the beach.

You're dead. Or you might as well be to everyone but me. When I wake late at night and I feel down the side of the wall in the dark hallway on the way to the bathroom I think about the wart on the side of your navel, how your eyes are soft but you are sneering, how I want to lick my way slowly up your leg while you click from ad to ad.

You're stupid. Your face shuts when I'm talking to you and you set the cup down with such finality in the saucer. This makes me want to take your fingernails and bend them back until your face turns white, until you bleed.

You punched me awake one morning because you thought I was faking sleep. This makes me wish I was there when you were weak and wasting away in the hospital needing, say, a little plastic cup of water I could withhold.

You're what I want. Your stretched out T-shirts, your change on the side of
the dresser.

You will always be a car ride down an unlit gravel road at midnight in
December, the half-smudged tree branches turning to undulating pylons,
the streetlamps like flat dead eyes.

And just when I'm lost, the car lurches to the left and lifts up and here I am all
of a sudden in my own driveway—a fool, a user, cold, dead, stupid—home.

SOME KIND OF SMALL YELLOW FLOWER

We were driving to your parents
through the pine woods of Mississippi
when you suddenly veered the car
onto a small dirt road
in a cleft between the blue trees
and we went into a field of tall weeds
with broad sheltering leaves
and some kind of small yellow flower
and we parked there,
two large walnut trees shading us,
their leaves twitching in the sky.
I climbed right on top of you
and you had my hips to guide
but my ass kept hitting the radio
making it change stations—
from Patsy Cline to Metallica
to Johnny Lee Hooker—
and the window was halfway open
so my small gurgles
went out to where the grasshoppers
sat chewing and staring
on their pulpy stalks.
And when you were done
we heard men talking
and I climbed off and we got out of there fast,
spinning back onto the blacktop,
driving the long way

to that pink house in New Orleans,
nothing to say on the causeway
over Lake Pontchartrain.
The road was the color of a dried-out worm
and we were done talking.
You were the most beautiful
man I had ever seen.
We knew where we were going—
smell of rot, swathes of swamp—
but it was worth it.

We Slept Naked

on a Zen mat
in Motel 6 just north of Tucson with a bullet-proof glass-windowed
   check-in desk
on an army cot in Fort Drum

we slept naked

in a rental car out in the Black Rock Desert
in a hospital where you were taken for observation after you saw angels on
   the F train
under pigeon-encrusted telephone wires

we slept naked

after tripping on acid and you seeing me as lava bubbling
as a blue-hooded cobra
as shapes jagged glass scattered lit-up jewelry

we slept naked

with the crime bars pushed open to car alarms and bats
with the telephone's red eye blinking
with the friend who stroked me with one hand and punched me with
   the other

with stoplights illuminating empty intersections
the strewn litter of stars
the night like a tarry parking lot emptied of paying customers

we slept naked

our dreams tucked away in boxes like old shoes
wrapped in plastic like old coats
stacked like old magazines

we slept naked

in our socks and hats
transparent spangled nylon
graduate school T-shirts
Superman underwear
with our pierced bejeweled nipples

we slept naked

always sleep naked

II.

SUBLIMATION

We lived in a flimsy stucco house in Missouri

and we rolled emptily in it like marbles thrown in a shoebox—my mother
   tangled and clear like a cat's eye, my father sparkly as crackled glass, me a
   small black sphere.

In the center was a long hallway with unloved white walls, new gray carpet,
   aluminum blinds covering one window. My mother worked all day and my
   father stayed at the room at the very end and even at two I knew not to cry.

The window was open and the hollow plastic knob on the end of the blind's
   string undulated like a bobber on wind-ruffled water

and there was a square of light on the rug showing the pure motes in the dust
   thick air and setting each hair of that rug on fire.

I didn't dare touch the fire. It taught me to love.

What Happened to Me

In third grade I raised my hand. All around me children were bent, blond and brown and long-haired, onto small scarred desks, cheeks crumpled onto sheets of ruled paper, mouths open, hands tracing cursive *o*'s and *s*'s. I could smell despair, which is the smell of dust and no moving air, no windows open, heaviness rising from the carpet. The teacher nodded and I went upstairs. The bathroom was dazzling white and mint green, windows cracked, fresh with Lysol, empty. First I sat down on the cold tile and saw how under the sink the pipes were fogged. Looking up I saw the lacy tops of trees and the playground. I pried the windows open wider and I held onto the gritty sill and lifted first one leg out then my small solid body followed and I sat on the ledge, the bushes three feet below me. The concrete was puddled and the jungle gym dew-dripped, each railing bright with beads of wet. I jumped. What happened to me? Long car rides up Highway 71 to the child psychiatrist's office in the city. I was punished. Half of me learned to stay crumpled over the white paper too. But the other half still hangs from ledge and sill, the wind stirring my skirt, the slide empty as an open hand.

RITALIN

It's hard to get comfortable with 107 electrodes implanted in your scalp.
You try not to think of tadpoles thickening ponds,
yeasty fruit flies in test tubes, frogs slit nose to crotch.
You see brightly colored ladders spinning on TV.
You see your head in MRI. Red blossoms.
Black holes where. He points with a yellow wand.
Young lady, he says. They say they can read your thoughts
so you try not to think about how much you love your mother
and hate her boyfriend's red hands. Meanwhile you find peace
in the way the blue mulberries saturate the sidewalk,
electric green lawns wide and still as a painted wall.

The teacher keeps your yellow pills in her pocket.
In five years all Americans will be using the metric system,
she says, the line where her makeup meets her skin
blurred with finger-marks, a new heavy book open
in her hands, her rings abundant and bright.

They Must Have Crawled in There to Get Warm

I don't know what my mom was baking that morning—I want it to be cookies
    for obvious reasons—but she set the oven to preheat

and left the room to read *Dr. Zhivago* while I rearranged the glass animals on
    the sun-struck bookshelf in my room

and she smelled frying ham and thought one of the neighbors was cooking
    and snuggled down deeper in the chair, wiggling her feet in her socks,

and the burning turned sticky-smelling, like hair, and she set her book down
    and walked to the kitchen

and inside the oven she saw, inside the black cast-iron frying pan, five hairless
    little mice lined up in nursing formation against their cooking mother,

and, maybe because that house was an oven cooking us too, she pulled them
    hard and liver-colored out

and buried them all under the maple sapling in the side yard, the one she fed
    all kinds of mulch.

ADOLESCENCE

Boys in gloves but with their coats off,
bent under the tumbled engines of their cars,
a mess of tools in their cracked driveways.
Nestled deep in the bushes by the railroad tracks,
I watched them like it was the world's first season.
Delicate in their dirty jeans.
Their necks, so bare in the cold.
I was afraid,
half a block away, far from home.

NEWLY GREEN FIELDS

My seventh grade teacher, Mr. Prehm,
told us how our parents
burnt a retarded black man to death
on the roof of a schoolhouse
because a young teacher
said she was violated.
He said the mob grabbed the man
from the sheriff's loose arms,
and carried him to the crowd
in the tall grass adjacent
the small white building,
how the goldenrod was in bloom,
how some people brought babies.
His voice thrilled over the man's guttural cries,
his arms raised in flames.
Whether our teacher was happy
to tell us what rednecks we were
or whether he was just happy
to describe a body burning,
the bones left, we couldn't tell.
I have seen the charred building,
a skeleton at the crossroads
of two worn tractor paths.
The wide field beside it blushes
with new pink clover,
mown by a man riding a Deere,
the sun warm as a genial
and lax hand on his shoulder.

Domestic Shorthair

Dad in his easy chair watching *Family Feud*

red elbow   doily   scarred wood   college essays   Cutty Sark

Jackie Gleason on a floodlit stage in a plaid suit

Mom pressed drying between the leaves of an enormous dictionary

our cat Diana eating from a lurid plastic dish

her sister Vesta scratching under the shadowy lilac

each heart-shaped leaf furry and black

and me under the headphones

a glittery stranger singing *I love you I love you I love you*

Take This Old Coat

Take this old coat,
it was my grandpa's,
and it's hung empty on this hook
for nearly ten years untouched,
but it's thick and it's warm
and it's already torn
so you don't have to be careful.
Take his gloves too.
We'll be going through brambles.
And his work boots.
He'd walk the muddy fields in those
with his slow-moving thick-hocked animals—
but he wouldn't be watching them,
he'd be looking for birds.
He loved to watch them flock
low and dark in the trees.
The dust off God's coat, he'd say.
Follow me on this tractor path
down here to the pond's banks,
down to this bramble.
Now look at the sky,
white as the underside of a fish.
But don't bother looking for birds.
It's too early.
So why are we here?
He was just another decent man.
That's rare enough.

And this farm?
He bought forty acres
and then he had a son—
and the story you heard about Grandpa
paying the doctor in potatoes
at Uncle Wayne's birth is true—
and then he had five more sons
and then he bought forty more acres
and forty more
and three died in war.
There's nothing different about this story.
This is where I used to go when I was a kid.
I was lonely and you don't need to know why.
I'd walk down here in his wool plaid coat,
the pockets gritty with sunflower seeds
and I'd squat on these
banks and watch the dimming sky
and the robins thickening the trees.
Once at dawn he took me out on his tractor.
The fields were frozen
but a warm blush was rising
and on the low scattered bushes
I saw the first birds.
They fluttered and rose
and I said, *Why do they fly?*
He had a harsh and joyous laugh.
Because they can, he said.
Pay attention.
When we go back in
shake off your boots first,
don't make Grandma sweep your dirt,

and when you go to the mudroom
let the clear water run in the deep and rust-scarred sink
until the steam rises up white and thick.
That room's cold as hell,
but that's what it's there for,
to make you fit to join the rest of us.

SOMETIMES A CAT LICKS A MOUSE

Our cat Eloise used to catch mice and bring them inside, still kicking in her black-gummed mouth. She'd prowl the corners of the living room, yowling for her kittens to come out of hiding. They never came because we had her fixed the day Dad left. *It's just hormonal,* the vet said. Sometimes my mother would pretend to be a kitten, rolling on the floor, the undersides of her white feet tender in the air.

GIRL DUMPED BY THE RIVER

Your body, soft and boneless,
like leaves or feathers,
cold water swirling under you
in a white froth, in dark pockets.
Your fingers white mushrooms,
the soles of your feet the pale
undersides of leaves.
Watch the clouds.
Tender hands gather them up,
pull them in a dark knot,
thread them through the sun.
You're something insects run through,
your eyes gray as grubs,
your smile a wasp hive,
your throat a dark den
of burrowing eyeless things,
you're mulch.

Driving My Grandmother to
Her Husband's Burial

It was misting when I looked outside.
The yellow grass tufted up tall
under thickets of trees thin and brambly
and the hilly fields and shallow ponds lay still.
I put the wipers on low.
Their arms shadowed the window.
She must have had some sight left
because she asked, *Are those birds?*
But it was too early for that.
There'd be more slow and overcast days
until the first small brown birds
came to mass in the trees.
She'd remember the way they lift up together,
all shadow and heft,
over the freshly plowed fields,
the outbuildings,
her empty and uncurtained room.

THE NORTH PLACE

the orange sky   like water boiling in a pot
keeps rolling in on itself   driving past
the trees like long wavy hair uncoiling
every night I'd stand on the crest of field
looking out onto the interstate passing the small town
fences wire and lush weeds   fist-sized rabbits
thinking of leaving was like losing your hand
in a man's thick hair   cars hurl ahead
the farm women stepping from their gardens
are undifferentiated outlines of scarves and skirts
any lit window could be the one

III.

THE ONE BLESSED THING

park here on the side of the gravel road
dust silvery in the strong sun
low hills of corn sparse trees
sky a bleached sheet fluttering down

pass through this gate
not wrought iron barbed wire
come to the graveyard
twenty headstones

lay your blanket out
on the long dry grass
the white clover
the hard wet walnut hulls

this baby is yours as much as mine
open your shirt to him
pull him sweaty and squirming
small as a kitten against your skin

look my grandmother's headstone
look my grandfather's headstone
the mulberry heavy sodden
fruit smeared and blackening on the roots

they wanted to see their farm
the house gone the barns razed
corn blowing white and green
where the roses used to be

he's your son too your beautiful son
he curls his legs
and the dead whir the trees
my dead drop the fruit
your dead turn the leaves

bring me that blue jay's feather
bring me that black-eyed Susan
from the dozen at the fence row
bring me the one blessed thing
I can hold in my hands forever

PERDITION

I am responsible for everything. I am powerless. I am a mother, a wife, deaf in one ear. I sit on the park bench, watching preteens push each other on swings. They are louder than children and their screams are real. Meaning, without joy. Their screams make all the adults look up and, in unison, leave.

CALLING

Walking in August,
the burnt leaves
still climbing their portion
of chain-link fence,
my son scrambling,
a waist-high blur.
The stranger's voice
is old and neighborly
and she is telling me
about her own grown son
who lives in a group home.
I picture her in an arm chair,
stained and worn and floral,
the room somber, a runner of sun
seeping through the shut blinds
and crawling up her hall.
At two he was normal, she says,
then he started going off
by himself in the corner,
he started doing weird things.
I have videos with him before,
trailing after my older girls.
My daughters watch
the tapes all the time
but I can't. He's my son.
Inside the playground
my own son steers clear

of the crowded sandbox,
dragging a stick across a fence,
circling the monkey bars.
The light shifts
in the trees, going blue,
shadows spreading
across the gravel.
I picture her walking
to her window and opening it
onto a yard dry and yellow
but filled with leaves.

NINE PLANETS

#1

Can he communicate his needs?
                I say *Shhh*, gesturing with my eyes.
                Three feet away my son chatters, shuttling dolls in their cardboard house.
It doesn't matter, the doctor says. *Can he ask for a glass of water?*

#2

First I sit on the bench in front of the empty playground—
                dark asphalt, still swings, monkey bars dripping.
           I don't know why you torment yourself, my husband says.
Then I watch dogs lunging after sticks thrown into water.

#3

Under waking birds
                sunrise splashes on brownstones,
           hurled and broken against brick walls.

#4

The trees are white by midmorning.
    Each leaf is urgently talking
  but there are so many leaves

#5

I can't—

#6

to *just accept it* would be like saying this world with its trees and mailboxes is
just like a skin which can be pulled off to reveal sky underneath stripped of
stars terrifying monochromatic directionless perfect

#7

I put glow-in-the-dark-stars on his walls
    so he won't be afraid at night,
  planets on his ceiling.
He names them—

*My Cherry, Vena, Birth, Margaret, Cupider, Pattern, Fire Anus, Necklace
Tune, Cute-o.*

#8

In the clinic preschoolers reach through the bars of a safety gate to take candy
from an unmanned reward cart.

#9

I tricked him into getting an MRI.
       I told him it was a space shuttle.
   He asked, *Where am I going?*

PAGEANT

Most of us come from work,
sitting alone with our stenciled
programs, the Special Ed
classroom awash in gray light,
the linoleum spackled and marked
from the dance of dirty feet.
The first group comes in,
white and brown kids
dressed in red and green—
some with Santa hats atilt,
some can shake the bells
they hold in their hands,
some blink confused
wondering how they got here,
some sit down, some cry,
some spin in circles.
Some start to sing.
It's the sound of sixteen bands
playing sixteen different songs
all at once and some of us
laugh but some—I see a mother
from my son's class break
from her chair—leave to cry
in private in the bathroom
or among the coats hung in the closet.
My son's class is led in.
I see my son as if he's in

a needle of light, his tousle
of blondish hair, as he sits
down cross-legged in the middle
of "Let It Snow, Let It Snow, Let It Snow"
and starts to eat his paper fan.
I want to go and stand among the coats
when he sees me and breaks
from the line to run.
He throws his bony arms
and knees into my lap and I smell
his shirt and hair and hold him,
not letting him get back in line,
not even when he wants to.

PORTAL

locked in the small blue room with the other strange boys

the books you are forced to read full of lies

pictures of obedient children with no faces behind their terrifying smiles

the worst among you already know how to act like that

on one wall a grayed two-way mirror dark as a wet rock

blank as the lake behind the stadium

you stop there after school on dying winter afternoons

waiting for one more layer of night to fall

the mirror is a portal

it makes the room bearable

pencil shavings lined up on your leg

shadow faces slithering on the other side of the glass

like fish darting

smudges in viscous water

STANZAS FOR MY SON

The way you laugh,
like the wind knocking a tree
into the side of a house.
You still have to ask, *Is she joking?*
We can't move the tree,
the wind, or our house,
so it grows that way
and the sound lives with us so long
we come to ignore it,
or at least we think we do.

*

The leaves are transparent
at first, small as fingernails,
but when a tree grows
taller than a fence post
or a man's shoulders,
they deepen nearly blue.

*

The eucalyptus
outside your nursery window

fills the entire pane,
a silver-green wall.
Its deep branches
blow against the shutters,
its bare open arms
so mother-like—
a mother forced to watch
her baby sigh and turn
through brittle glass,
helplessly crooning
nursery rhymes
terrifying in their sweetness.

*

We visited a friend
who lived in the country
and he showed us
his apple tree.
These are wild apples,
he said. *Not like what you get*
at the grocery store.
They were warped
and white-green,
small as walnuts.
You gathered them
when it got dark,
running towards the house
with apples bundled

in your shirt
but when you got in
you put them on the table
and forgot about them.
I left them out
on the porch
for the deer.
Where are my apples, Mother,
you said when
it was time to leave,
What did you do with them?

*

Just this morning's walk up
a gravel road. Lavish and hairy
weeds wet with morning mist,
the pale blue flame of chicory
tipping spindly stalks, the smell
of new growth and rot and sun.
This life, so redolent and stark.
You'd split open if you stopped.

A Mask

I slip the thin string of elastic over my child's head when my thumb grazes his
    cheek soft as water.

My husband holds him down on the floor as I lift his head, pulling the strings
    tighter, knotting the back.

A mask hard as cardboard, thick as an egg carton with a line of gleaming
    staples running up each cheek,

painted bone-white with black lines like the fissures of a skull.

There are two perfect circles where his eyes should be.

We insist he wear it over his real face just for you.

Pulsar over Hoyt-Schermerhorn

"I like it that order exists somewhere even if it shatters near me."—Elizabeth Moon, *Speed of Dark*

This is the book where life is changed and everything is new again,

where we walk astonished beside the towers, a spray of white birds hurling straight up into the sky.

This is the book where in the last chapter I don't care that I love you more than I comprehend you,

where they cure everybody and I meet you on the sidewalk and I can make sense of what you're saying,

and we come inside together and I roast birds and give you my skin and you let me tuck the small blanket furry and black under your chin,

and you look past me at the one pulsar, red and blue as a cop car's light, its scintillation of radio waves low over the street,

and you don't talk about gravitational radiation, it's just a star to you because you are someone else.

This is the book where terrible changes happen but our mouths are radiant.

This is the book we read in the kind of afternoon that stretches out long as life.

IV.

CUTTING

It's a book you wear,
each page curled around you
until the paper becomes your skin,
the writing tattoos you make.
Some are made with safety pins,
delicate and pinkish, a filigree of scratches
lacing the insides of your thighs.
Some are made with razors,
wrist cuffs and ankle bracelets,
bold lines of barbed wire,
the crisscross like a corset's lacing.
And some are the snowflake splotches
of cigarette burns—
your belly a blizzard,
your hips a soft drifting field.
You try to cover them up
with long sleeves and scarves.
But your secret wants a reader.

QUILT

Tell me a story, you say.

I refuse to tell you the story.

Tell me a story, I say.

He just met a woman and he was crazy about her, you say.

But the boy pursued too ardently and the woman stopped picking up the phone and the boy was sad.

Then she called back, I say.

I won't line the pieces up because this isn't a photo album or a quilt or cooking.

Once my ex-husband was fucking me in the bathtub and when I choked on water I saw him smile.

Right now I love you, you say.

All this doesn't mean I don't like sex, by the way.

I even like the part about being crushed.

Especially.

Today: skeins of leaves in the streets.

Once upon a time a bride stood so close to the candles that the baby's breath
in her bouquet caught on fire.

At my grandfather's funeral my grandmother said *I thought we would take that
journey together.*

I drove her to the cemetery. It was March, forsythia. Broken rows of rotted
fence lined the highway. Mist. The wipers on low. Their shadows drifted.
Are those birds?

A year later they sewed her lips shut with plastic.

Once upon a time a husband got out the wedding keepsake photo album and
took the pink and unblinking faces of baby dolls cut out of magazines and
glued them on top of his own.

Once upon a time she wore his dead grandmother's ring, just to be polite.

Once before a wedding someone clogged the toilet in the church. Bending
down the bride-to-be saw her stepfather's wallet spread out across the tile.

Last night I dreamt my ex put my father's heart on a plate and I ate it.

When I woke you were sleeping and I covered you with my grandmother's
quilt,

a pattern called Double Wedding Ring, made from all the leftover pink at the
bottom of her sewing basket.

THE GRIEVING

Our torsos are translucent,
each like a china bowl held to light;

our ribs are the shadows of fingers
visible through the glass,

the heart a red stew inside.
We get old, growing gentler with understanding,

gentler and more helpless.
We don't want to eat,

but we are polite guests on earth
and bend to the dark broth in the spoon.

The Rival

There was a time I set out to destroy myself the way one would a rival.

I had an apartment with only one window that looked onto a parking lot.

Other people were candles scattered around a bleak room.

Some sputtered out.

Some were tossed still smoking.

I watched myself the way an impeccably dressed woman watches a drunk at a party, a little smirk on my face.

She deserves it, I said.

I hate her coffee, her pimpled ass.

I'm sick of her sobbing, slamming doors, vomiting.

One night she even followed a man onto a subway at 3 a.m.

Please, she said,

to the fluorescent lighting

to the orange seat

to the woman reading a paperback.

Oh, please.

She'd turn up the music loud and empty herself into drinking.

That meant she still had a self to empty.

Take that, I said.

At night we lay with our ex, coupled hip to thigh under the patchy mosquito
netting, wandering empty and lost.

His parking lot. Mine.

Here's the dusky store filled with legless mannequins.

Here's the dumpster swirled with rats.

Here's the razor-wired moon.

I watched you spiral down, he said, *and it hasn't been pretty.*

Her face was pretty wrecked.

Puffy eyes,

broken capillaries.

And all that witch's hair.

I smeared lipstick on her fanged smile.

I hid her hairy feet in velvet slippers.

Now someone loves her.

He gave her platinum.

He gave her seven sapphires, bezel-cut.

I closed her clawed heart up in a little locket

but she shone like a pocketful of coins.

Anywhere I'd Want to Be

After twelve years
away in the city
I climbed the stairs
to a room they said
was mine. I smelt dust
and something sweet
under the dust,
like drying apples.
Dead flies scattered
across the window sills.
I brushed them off
and lifted the latch.
It was early enough
that the sky was still
dark blue and I could
make out the dirt road,
rust colored at sunset,
and a field of pink clover,
two quarter horses
bowing down to the cricket's song,
the rattle from a passing pickup,
the spray of gravel.
I forgot this was anywhere
I wanted to be.
I stood in a semicircle
of desiccated flies,

the wind blowing the white
curtain back, some unseen light
catching this tattered life,
so it seemed to glow.

To My Analyst

Together we make a dress. This has taken us, so far, five years. For just one simple dress. Something to wear. First there's the problem of the pattern. We need to agree on that. Then there's getting the sewing kit together. You have the scissors and thread. But I'm the one who's supposed to supply the fabric. That was our deal. Every day I come in with something different. Something from outside. Something slick or something rough, something flowered or sequined or shiny, something to hide my hands in, something like absolute stillness. You get your scissors out and go to work. I watch you cutting into absolute stillness. Tiny little sections. I admire your work. Sewing the buttons on. This is the dress they'll bury me in. We made it. You'll say we worked on it together, but it was already made.

MULBERRY STREET

No matter where I am, I am always standing on this street.

It's luminous blue out so I think it must be getting dark.

But it could be getting light.

It could be the darkness lifting like a sheet being pulled slowly off a body

you don't want to see naked.

I'm ten, I'm twenty, I'm forty.

In the trees the wind-lashed shadows make it clear

there will be no help forthcoming.

In the lit-up kitchen I see my mother's back,

her sorrow, her neck bent like a shot bird's.

I should walk inside and touch her.

I should pick a small part of her—her scapula, say—

and love it through the gauzy amaryllis she calls her shirt.

But I am not that child.

I'm the child who scuffles amid brown leaves and bracken buried all winter,

in love with the cold streetlight.

Acknowledgments

Some of these poems have appeared, at times in different versions, in the following publications:

Agni, "Ritalin"
Atlanta Review, "Sublimation"
Blue Earth Review, "Edge," "Some Kind of Small Yellow Flower"
Calyx, "Take This Old Coat"
Cream City Review, "You"
Diner, "Blind Date," *"Let Me Blindfold You"*
Faultline, "Cutting"
Grand Street, "The North Place"
Great Midwestern Quarterly, "It Is Beautiful"
Harpur Palate, "White Gold"
Hayden's Ferry Review, "They Must Have Crawled in There to Get Warm," "To My Analyst"
Lake Effect, "Girl Dumped by the River"
Michigan Quarterly Review, "Mulberry Street"
New Delta Review, "The Grieving"
Pebble Lake Review, "The One Blessed Thing"
Plastic Ocean, "We Slept Naked" (formerly "We Sleep Naked")
Poetry Daily, "Mulberry Street"
Rhino, "Blue Curve of Empty Interstate"
Tusculum Review, "Quilt"

Some of these poems also appeared in the chapbook *Edge*, which was selected for the Center for Book Arts Poetry Chapbook Competition judged by David St. John and published by the Center for Book Arts in 2014.

"You" was selected by Josh Bell for *Cream City Review*'s 2008 Beau Boudreaux Poetry Prize.

I would like to thank the Vermont Studio Center and the Virginia Center for the Creative Arts for their support in the completion of this book.

Additional thanks to Kim Addonizio, Paula Bohince, Susan Brennan, Jennifer Chapis, and Robert Huddleston, and everyone in my writers groups in San Francisco and New York.

And special thanks to David Lincoln and my mom.